D0590291

Aberdeenshire
3065536

ABERDEENSHIRE LIBRARY & INFO SERV	
3065536	
Bertrams	17/02/2012
J551.457	£10.99

A World of Field Trips

Going to a Beach

Rebecca Rissman

www.raintreepublishers.co.uk
Visit our website to find out more information about Raintree books.

To order:
Phone 0845 6044371
Fax +44 (0) 1865 312263
Email myorders@raintreepublishers.co.uk

Customers from outside the UK please telephone +44 1865 312262

Raintree is an imprint of Capstone Global Library Limited, a company incorporated in England and Wales having its registered office at 7 Pilgrim Street, London, EC4V 6LB – Registered company number: 6695582.

Text © Capstone Global Library Limited 2012
First published in hardback in 2012
The moral rights of the proprietor have been asserted.

All rights reserved. No part of this publication may be reproduced in any form or by any means (including photocopying or storing it in any medium by electronic means and whether or not transiently or incidentally to some other use of this publication) without the written permission of the copyright owner, except in accordance with the provisions of the Copyright, Designs and Patents Act 1988 or under the terms of a licence issued by the Copyright Licensing Agency, Saffron House, 6–10 Kirby Street, London EC1N 8TS (www.cla.co.uk). Applications for the copyright owner's written permission should be addressed to the publisher.

Edited by Rebecca Rissman, Dan Nunn, and Catherine Veitch
Designed by Richard Parker
Picture research by Tracy Cummins
Originated by Capstone Global Library Ltd
Printed and bound in China by Leo Paper Products Ltd

ISBN 978 1 406 23515 9
16 15 14 13 12 11
10 9 8 7 6 5 4 3 2 1

British Library Cataloguing in Publication Data
Rissman, Rebecca.
Going to a beach. -- (World of field trips)
551.4'57-dc22

Acknowledgements
We would like to thank the following for permission to reproduce photographs: Corbis pp. 16 (© TWPhoto), 17 (© John Stanmeyer/VII), 20 (© moodboard); Getty Images pp. 5 (Hans Neleman), 15 (Darren Robb), 18 (Macduff Everton), 21 (Coto Elizondo); istockphoto pp. 4 (© Sean Locke), 6 (© David Cannings- Bushell), 9 (© ra-photos), 10 (© Jay Spooner), 23d (© ra-photos); Shutterstock pp. 7 (© Vinicius Tupinamba), 8 left (© Dominik Michálek), 8 right (© Cees Nooij), 11 (© BlueOrange Studio), 12 (© Joyce Marrero), 13 (© Connie Lanyon-Roberts), 14 (© oliveromg), 19 (© Yuri Arcurs), 22 (© Jan Kranendonk), 23a (© Cees Nooij), 23b (© oliveromg), 23c (© Dominik Michálek).

Front cover photograph of children running on a beach reproduced with permission of Photolibrary (Denis Debadier/ Photononstop). Back cover photograph of a rocky beach reproduced with permission of Shutterstock (© Joyce Marrero).

Every effort has been made to contact copyright holders of any material reproduced in this book. Any omissions will be rectified in subsequent printings if notice is given to the publisher.

Contents

Field trips 4

Field trip to a beach 6

Different beaches 10

How should you behave at
the beach? 20

What do you think? 22

Picture glossary 23

Index 24

Field trips

People go on field trips to visit new places.

People go on field trips to learn new things.

Field trip to a beach

Some people go on field trips to beaches.

A beach is near the water.

Some beaches are covered in pebbles. Some beaches are covered in sand.

Most sand is made of tiny pieces of rocks and shells.

Different beaches

This beach has black sand.

The sand gets hot in the sun!

This beach is rocky.

The waves crash against the rocks.

Be careful!

This beach has sand dunes.

You can climb up the sand dunes.

This beach is made by humans.

The people put sand here for you to enjoy.

This beach has white sand.

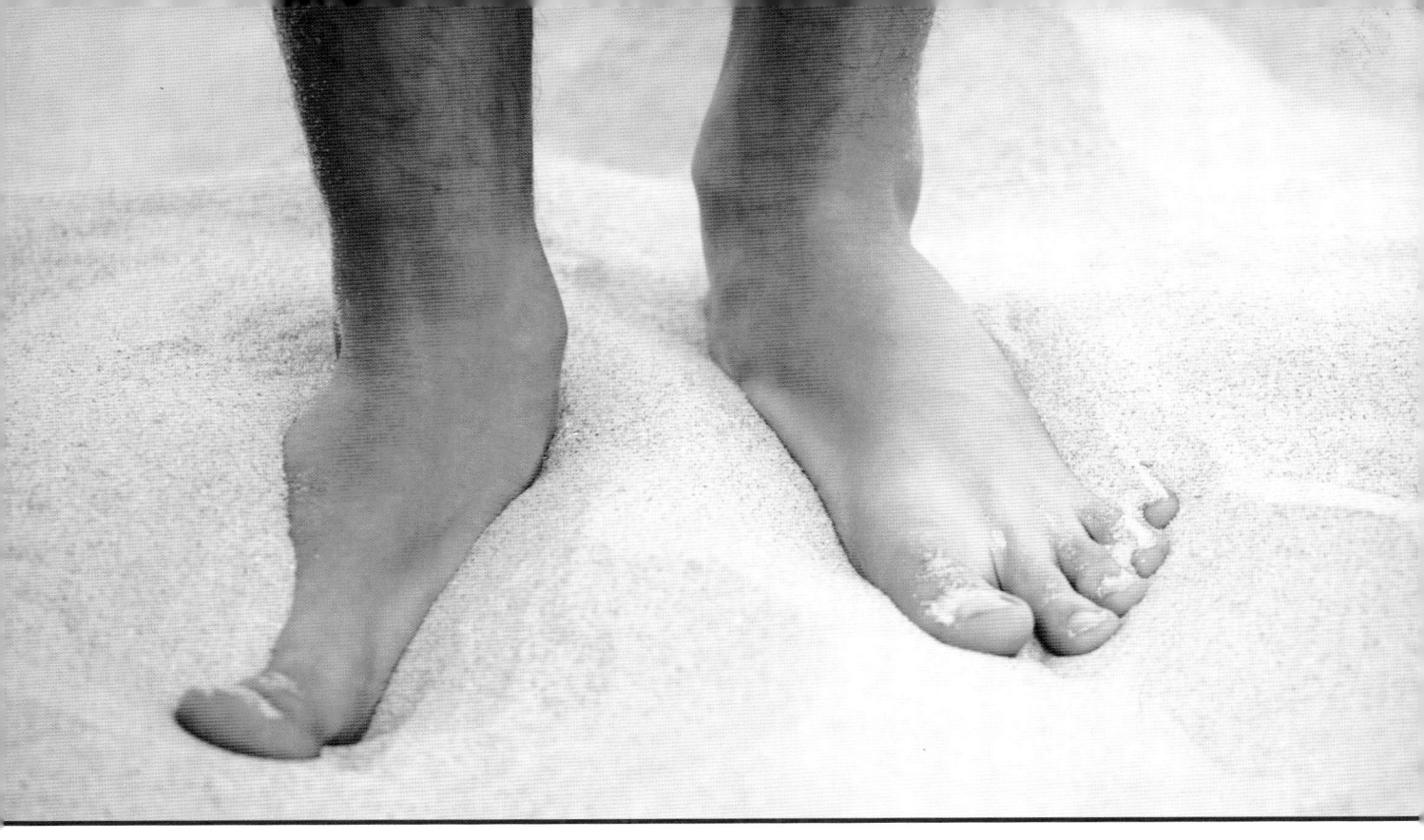

You can press your toes into the warm sand.

How should you behave at the beach?

Always wear suncream at the beach.

Only swim when adults are nearby.

What do you think?

What kind of beach is this?

Look on page 24 for the answer.

Picture glossary

beach area of land near lakes, oceans, or seas. A beach can be sandy or rocky.

dune hill of sand. Sand dunes can be very large.

pebble small rock

sand tiny pieces of rock and shells that can be found on beaches

Index

black sand 10
pebbles 8, 23
rocks 9, 12, 13
sand 8, 9, 10, 11, 17, 18, 19, 23
sand dunes 14, 15, 23
suncream 20
waves 13
white sand 18

Notes for parents and teachers

Before reading
Explain to children that a field trip is a short visit to a new place, and that it often takes place during a school day. Ask children if they have ever taken a field trip. Show children the front cover of the book and ask them if they know what landform the cover shows. Explain to them that it is a beach, and that beaches are the areas of land near water. Some beaches are covered in pebbles, while others are covered in sand.

After reading

- Show children the images on pages 10–11, and then compare them with the images on pages 18–19. Explain to children that the sand is different colours because it is made of different materials. The black sand beach comes from black volcanic rock. The white sand comes from light-coloured shells and stones.
- Remind children to practise good water safety when they are at the beach. Have children brainstorm a list of good safety tips, and make a "Beach Safety" poster to hang in the classroom. Remember to include items such as only swimming when adults are near.

Answer to page 22
It is a pebble beach.